D0364898

Coral Reefs
in Danger

by Samantha Brooke
illustrated by Peter Bull

Random House 🏠 New York

It is morning. The sun
rises over the ocean.
Something is poking out
of the water. It looks like
a tree branch. But it is
not a tree branch.

It is coral. Below the
waves is a busy world—the
world of a coral reef.

A coral reef is home to many creatures. Thousands of different small fish live here. So do sharks, eels, and octopuses. Whales and sea turtles also come to visit.

Coral reefs grow

in warm, salty water.

On this map, coral reefs are in red.

Most are near the equator in shallow

water.

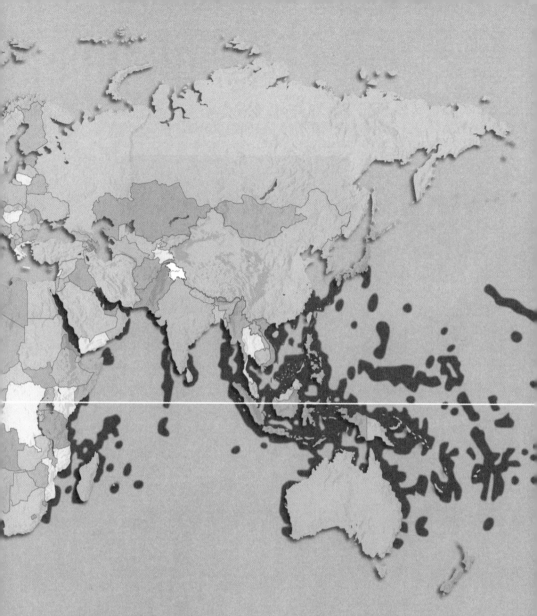

That's because a coral reef needs
lots of sunlight. Deep water is too
dark and cold for most forms
of coral.

9

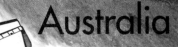

Great Barrier Reef

Australia

The largest reef is off the coast
of Australia. The Great Barrier
Reef stretches for over 1,250 miles.
Astronauts can see it from space!

But if coral isn't a rock, what exactly is it? Coral is an animal. The hard outside is the skeleton. Inside is the animal.

Lobsters and crabs also have skeletons on the outside.

A coral reef starts with one small polyp (say: POL-up). It attaches itself to a rock.

The polyp is shaped like a tube. Its mouth is at the top. Around the mouth are tiny tentacles that help catch food.

Over and over again a polyp sprouts new polyps. It is like a tree with new branches.

Coral grows very slowly. And it always stays in the same place.

A group of the same polyps is called a colony.

A colony can grow to be as big as a house. It can live for hundreds of years.

Not all coral colonies look the same.

cabbage coral

mushroom coral

cactus coral

Staghorn coral looks like deer
antlers. Mushroom coral looks
like the underside of
a mushroom.

finger coral

brain coral

Daytime is the best time to visit a coral reef. That's when colorful fish are out and about.

There are thousands of
different fish in a reef.

At night, colorful fish are in danger. Sharks, eels, rays, and octopuses come hunting for food.

Many fish hide deep in the reef.
Others swim to deeper water. That
doesn't stop sharks from hunting.

Sharks use their sense of smell to find food. But this white-tipped reef shark swims right by a parrot fish.

Why? The parrot fish has wrapped itself in a sticky bubble. The shark cannot smell it.

In the dark, an octopus
uses its eight arms to feel for
food. It has grabbed a crab.

But moray eels are also out at night. And they like to eat octopus! The eel attacks. It bites the octopus on one arm.

But the octopus can break
off its own arm! Now it is free.

It squirts out a cloud of dark ink.

This is its chance to escape.

Whoooosh! Off it goes!

At night, coral finds food. Out come its tentacles. The tentacles have poison stingers.

Back and forth they wave in the water. They trap tiny plants and animals floating by.

Then the sun rises. The coral tentacles go back inside the polyp. The colorful fish come out of hiding.

Another day begins in the life of the reef.

Coral reefs have existed for millions of years. They were around even before dinosaurs.

But they are more than just
beautiful homes for fish and plants.
Reefs help protect the shore from
storms. They provide food and
medicines.

But coral reefs are in danger! And
the enemy is us.

Boom!

Sometimes fishermen use dynamite to kill many fish at once. The blast can destroy a coral reef.

Pollution on shore can harm coral reefs and the fish who live there.

Fertilizers help crops grow. But fertilizers can seep into the ground and wash out to sea. They, too, harm coral reefs.

But perhaps the greatest danger to
reefs is global warming.

Global warming means that the
average temperature of the entire
Earth is increasing.

Have you heard of greenhouse gases? They are natural gases in the atmosphere. They form a layer around our planet.

Greenhouse gases help keep our planet nice and warm.

Just like the glass walls of a greenhouse, gases like carbon dioxide hold in heat from the sun.

But people have been adding more and more of these gases to the atmosphere.

How? We release these gases when

we drive cars . . .

We also release these gases when we use electricity, and when we heat or cool our homes.

The layer of greenhouse gases has

become too thick. Too much heat is trapped in the atmosphere.

This means the weather is warmer in many parts of our planet.

But what does global warming
have to do with coral reefs?
When the ocean is even a little bit
too warm, coral may bleach.

It turns ghostly gray or white.
Bleaching can be a sign that the
coral is about to die.

Scientists worry about the coral reefs.

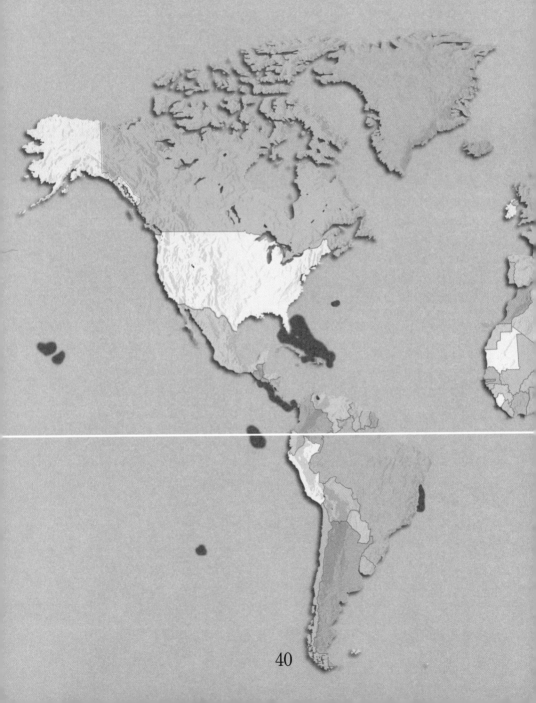

The green areas show coral reefs that are in danger. Up to one-third of the world's coral reefs have already died.

It is not too late to save coral reefs. It is not too late to stop global warming.

Here are some things you can do to help.

Ask your family to walk or ride bikes to places close by. Try to use less electricity. Remember to turn off lights.

In winter, use less fuel to heat your home. Wear a sweater indoors.

In summer, use less air-conditioning.
Open a window for a cool breeze.

Plant a tree! Trees remove carbon dioxide from the air. (Remember, carbon dioxide is one of the major greenhouse gases.)

Tree roots also hold on to soil. They stop too much sediment from getting into the ocean. Sediment makes the water too cloudy for coral to grow.

Coral reefs are truly one of the world's natural wonders. We must do our part to make sure that coral reefs will be around for millions of years to come.